This igloo book belongs to:

. . . .

igloobooks

Published in 2018
by Igloo Books Ltd
Cottage Farm
Sywell
NN6 0BJ
www.igloobooks.com

STA002 0418
6 8 10 9 7
ISBN 978-1-78343-654-5

Written by Elizabeth Dale
Illustrated by Natalia Moore

Printed and manufactured in China

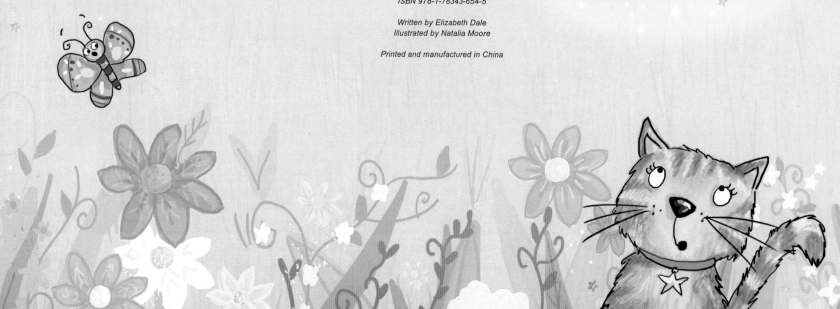

Written by Elizabeth Dale

OOPS-a-Daisy
Here comes Maisy!

Illustrated by Natalia Moore

igloobooks

The fairy friends of Cupcake Wood
were **happy** as could be.
They had such **fun** as they prepared
for Honey's birthday tea.

They worked for **hours**, dusting flowers and tidying away.

Then, they all cried, "Oh! We forgot that **Maisy's on her way!**"

Everyone loved Maisy, but whenever she was there...

...She bombed the fairy beehive and got honey in her hair.

When Maisy's spells made horrid smells, it really was a pain.

She made a spell for sunshine, but instead it poured with rain.

Maisy waved her magic wand
to make a gift for Honey.
The spell went **wrong**, she made a **mess**
and no one found it funny.

Then, Maisy flew into the woods.
"I won't use spells," she said.

"I'll try my best to use my skills
to make a gift, instead."

Soon, everything was ready for the birthday-party fun.
When Maisy zoomed in asking, "Has the party tea begun?"

The birthday gift for Honey slipped and landed with a **SPLAT!**

"Oops-a-daisy!" cried clumsy Maisy.

"How on earth did I do that?"

Cake splattered on the food, on sandwiches and sweets.
"Oh, no!" cried Maisy, sadly.
"Look, I've spoiled the birthday treats."

Poor Maisy felt so bad because she'd ruined Honey's day. "I'm sorry everyone!" she cried and quickly flew away.

"Oh, please don't go!" cried Honey,
as she wiped away a tear.
"I want you at my birthday tea... "

... but Maisy didn't hear.

The fairies mopped up all the mess and Honey dried her eyes.
She unwrapped Maisy's birthday gift and had a big surprise!

Inside, there was a pretty dress of gold and silver flowers. "Maisy made this," Honey said, "It must have taken **hours!**"

"Maisy can't do spells," said Honey.
"She always makes a mess.
Yet only someone **special**
could have made this lovely dress."

Each fairy's wings went droopy
and then Honey said, "I'm sad.

We've got to find poor Maisy, quick,
she must be feeling bad."

The fairies fluttered high and low,
in every glade and nook.

They found unhappy Maisy
on a toadstool with a book.

"Oh, there you are!" cried Honey.
"We've been looking everywhere.
We missed your crazy spells
and all the honey in your hair."

"I love my gift," said Honey. "Oh, please do come and play!
My party won't be any fun, if you stay away."

Maisy fluttered her little wings and giggled, happily.
"I'm so very glad," she said, "that you aren't cross with me."

Maisy laughed and had such fun and it was all because...

... her fairy friends in Cupcake Wood loved her, **just as she was.**